JOEL MADTHA

DETERMINED NOT DETERRED

THE LEADERSHIP YOU BUILD WHEN NO ONE'S WATCHING

BlueRose ONE.com
Stories Matter
NewDelhi • London

BLUEROSE PUBLISHERS
U.K.

BlueRose ONE.com
Stories Matter
NewDelhi • London

For permissions requests or inquiries regarding this publication,
please contact:

BLUEROSE PUBLISHERS
www.BlueRoseONE.com
info@bluerosepublishers.com
+4407342408967

ISBN: 978-93-7139-924-1

Cover design: Daksh
Typesetting: Tanya Raj Upadhyay

First Edition: December 2025

To my parents- Joseph & Juliana Madtha

Your words shaped my structure, but it was your silences that gave me strength. When life was unjust, you did not protest. You endured. You walked through storms with quiet dignity, unshaken in your values and unyielding in your courage. You never demanded anything in return, yet gave everything that mattered. Every page of this book carries your fingerprints, even if the world cannot see them.

To my family- Sangeeta Madtha, Diana & Mehul Gala, Jivan & Sukhminder Madtha, Samaira Gala and Aryan Madtha

You have held a mirror to every part of me: the flawed, the fragile, the restless, and the relentless. You have seen the laughter and the fire, the doubts and the drive. You've known the versions of me that no résumé could ever contain. Thank you for standing beside me through each reinvention, for believing not only in who I was but also in who I strive to become. Your love has been my quiet compass, the one constant that reminds me where I come from, no matter how far I go.

To Ron Morris, Shelley Morris, Itamar Gero, Ajay Aggarwal, Melissa Pangan, Gizelle Cabahug Fugoso, Brigadier Suresh Salokhe, Joshua Dass, Jeff Weigh, Joyce Casenas, Kevin Pinto, Sanjay Ponnappa, Maninder Kapoor Puri, Jeff Brown, Khushrav Patel, Tarit Kumar and Neil D'silva

You each came into my life at very different points, yet somehow left the same kind of mark, one that doesn't fade. What stays with me is not the positions we held or the work we did, but the way you believed in me when I hadn't fully figured myself out. You gave me space to grow, make mistakes, and still belong. Some of you brought me into your own worlds, your projects, your teams, your ideas and in doing so, you made me feel trusted in ways that shaped my confidence quietly, but permanently. I didn't just learn from you; I evolved beside you. And for that, my gratitude runs deeper than words can hold.

To Dr. Aarti Sharma and Dr. Bhupesh Manoharan, and to my mentors at Masters' Union

You expanded my understanding of business and leadership, but more importantly, you deepened my sense of purpose. You reminded me that knowledge is hollow without integrity, and that true learning begins when you start questioning your own certainties. Your lessons did not end in the classroom, they continue to shape how I see the world and my place in it.

To Benjie Francisco Espina

You didn't just help shape the message. You helped shape the journey. You questioned, refined, and challenged every idea until it found its right form. You made me see my own work through the lens of truth, not comfort. This book might still exist without you, but it would not speak with the same voice.

To Samaira Gala

Thank you for reading the entire book before anyone else did, and for ratifying its release with your early approval. That single act set the tone for me to move ahead with confidence. Your clarity, honesty, and quiet conviction gave this work its first moment of validation and that meant more than you know.

To Prashant Jagtap, Swebert Ralph D'Souza, Shiny D'Souza, and Allan D'Souza

Your quiet faith and thoughtful conversations found their way into my reflections more often than you know. You stood by me with understanding, not judgment, and reminded me that leadership is not about standing above others but growing alongside them. I carry your encouragement with humility and deep gratitude.

To the teammates and partners who chose the long road with me

You did not follow. You believed. You carried the weight when it was heavy, and you lifted the vision when it began to fade. You stood beside me when choices were difficult and moments were uncertain. This book carries traces of your spirit in every chapter. It belongs to you as much as it does to me.

To the people who left

Yes, even you. You gave me clarity. You made me recognize who I could not become and what I must never accept. Your absence was also a form of guidance, one that helped me draw my own boundaries and protect what matters most. I thank you, not out of bitterness, but with complete understanding.

To the invisible believers

The ones who sent quiet messages, who took an idea seriously before it was proven. You are the ones who reminded me that impact doesn't require millions. It requires meaning, and one genuine voice that says, "Keep going." You were that voice, often unseen but always felt.

To every reader holding this book

Whether you are leading in silence, rebuilding after betrayal, or simply trying to remain human in a world that often forgets what humanity feels like, I see you. I wrote this not as an expert but as someone who is still walking the same road, perhaps just a few steps ahead in certain places. Thank you for reading this with your heart open. Now go and build with your truth unfiltered, unguarded, and undeterred.

With all my respect,
Joel Madtha

Dedication

To the ones who stayed.

Through the silence.

Through the slow seasons.

Through the storm.

To the ones who didn't need headlines to believe.

Who held space when the world kept on changing.

Who reminded me that quiet strength is still strength.

To every overlooked leader still showing up.

To every believer still building with bare hands.

To every soul who chose character over comfort.

This is for you.

You are not alone.

You were never wrong to care this much.

- JM

Preface:
Before You Begin

This is not a self-help book.

It's not a leadership manual.

It's not a highlight reel.

It's a story - built from real pressure, real pain, and real principle.

A story of what it means to stay human in a world that constantly demands performance.

A story of walking into rooms where no one expects you to belong - and staying anyway.

A story of building things that matter, even when no one claps, no one sees, and nothing is certain.

I didn't write this book from the mountaintop.

I wrote it from the middle - from boardrooms and backrooms, from late nights and silent flights, from years of being misunderstood, displaced, tested, but never erased.

Each chapter was lived first, and written later.

If you're a leader who's tired of pretending you have it all figured out,

If you're someone who's navigating betrayal, burnout, or just quiet disappointment,

If you've ever been told to "toughen up" when all you really wanted was to stay tender and still succeed,

Then this book is for you.

Not to give you the answers.

But to affirm your instincts.

To sharpen your questions.

And to remind you:

You don't need to be louder.

You just need to stay true.

Every chapter ends with a deeper truth:

That you don't have to conform to lead.

You don't have to become cold to be taken seriously.

You don't have to chase noise to create impact.

You just have to stay in it - involved, not indifferent.

Present, not performative.

Determined. Not deterred.

So take a breath.

Set aside your filters.

And read this like it was written *for you.*

Because it was.

- *Joel Madtha*

Author, Builder, Believer

Involved Until Resolved

Prologue:
You Weren't Supposed to Read This

You weren't supposed to read this.

This was never meant to be a book. It was a journal - scribbled at 3 AM on sleepless nights, between meetings that drained me and moments that nearly broke me. Therapy, not literature. Survival, not strategy.

And yet, here you are. And here I am - letting you in. Because I realized I wasn't the only one navigating storms with a brave face and bleeding knuckles. I wasn't the only one told to "stay strong" when strength had long expired. I wasn't the only one building in the dark with no applause, no map, no margin for error.

This book is for the ones who don't quit. Even when they wanted to. Especially when they wanted to.

If you're holding this, maybe you're rebuilding. Maybe you've just been told no again - by someone, by life, by your own reflection.

I don't have magic words. But I do have this: You are allowed to be tired. You are allowed to be hurt. But you are not done. Because if you're still breathing, you're still building.

Determination means you're still in the fight - even if you don't feel brave right now. Not deterred means they didn't win.

Let's begin.

Table of Contents

Part I:
The Making:
Before the metrics, there was meaning.

Chapter 1: The Silence Before the Storm

Before there was resilience, there was routine.

Before there was purpose, there was pressure.

And before I ever learned how to fight, I learned how to stay silent.

I grew up in a world that didn't make noise unless it had to. A world of small rituals and unspoken expectations. The morning light slipping through curtains, the clink of steel tumblers, the subtle rhythm of a disciplined household. My father - an army veteran - didn't raise his voice. He didn't have to. His presence spoke what words couldn't. Order. Honor. Duty.

And in that stillness, I learned early that *discipline wasn't control - it was care in disguise.*

But I also learned how to hold things in. How to carry questions I wasn't sure I was allowed to ask. How to smile with curiosity and ache with ambition - quietly.

There was no grand tragedy. No dramatic explosion. Just the **slow, invisible formation of hunger**. A hunger not for rebellion, but for *reach* - to stretch beyond my zip code, my surname, and the quiet lines I'd been taught not to cross.

I became obsessed with understanding people - why they acted the way they did, how they made choices, how they masked fears with titles, smiles, or silence. I'd listen more than I spoke. Watch more than I reacted. I didn't know it then, but I was slowly becoming a strategist - not of war or business, but of *human nature.*

In school, I wasn't the loudest. But I noticed everything. The teacher who gave up halfway through the lesson. The friend who cracked jokes to hide his anxiety. The systems - spoken and unspoken - that decided who got seen and who got sidelined.

I didn't resent it. I just logged it. Filed it into a mind that was always working - not loudly, but relentlessly.

And that's what most people miss about resilience. It doesn't start with a fall.

It starts in the silence.

In the tension between who you are and who you're expected to be.

In the silent promises you make to yourself before the world gives you a reason to speak them out loud.

Looking back, I realize the storm didn't come suddenly. It had always been there - in the quiet rooms, the suppressed dreams, the decisions made for me before I even knew I could say no.

But this chapter isn't about the storm. It's about the *awareness before the thunder* - the moment you realize you were built for something more, even if you can't name it yet.

It's the moment your spirit starts whispering what your voice hasn't yet found the courage to say.

And for me, that whisper was clear:

"You will not be deterred. Not by silence. Not by tradition. Not even by yourself."

Chapter 2: When the World Says No

The first big "no" - and how it cracked my sense of safety but revealed your deeper core.

You never forget your first *No*.

Not the polite rejection letters. Not the emails that begin with "unfortunately."

I mean the kind of 'no' that *undoes you* - that scrapes against your identity and whispers, "Maybe you're not enough."

Mine came wrapped in formality and logic.

Well-dressed. Well-reasoned. Brutally reasonable.

And for a while, I believed it.

I had done everything right - or so I thought. I followed the path laid out like train tracks: good grades, a steady job, respect for systems older than me. I believed that merit spoke louder than anything else.

What no one told me was that **systems don't reward quiet excellence**. They reward compliance, connections, and well curated confidence. And if you come from a background where humility is prized, where elders are never challenged, and where dreams are quiet so they don't wake reality - you enter the world *unarmed*.

I was unarmed, too.

Not intellectually. Not emotionally. But *politically*.

I walked into corporate life expecting fairness. What I got was hierarchy, ego, and unwritten rules - rules I hadn't been trained to play by.

The rejection wasn't just of a job or opportunity. It was rejection of identity.

It was a moment where I had to choose: **Will I fold, or will I forge?**

I'll be honest. At first, I folded. I withdrew. Questioned everything. Maybe I wasn't smart enough. Maybe I wasn't polished enough. Maybe I wasn't "global" enough. I remember staring at the mirror and wondering if this - this invisible wall - would be permanent.

That's when I learned the truth no one wants to admit:

The world doesn't always say no because you're not good enough. Sometimes it says no because you don't fit the version of success it's comfortable with.

And if you're building a new path - if your success doesn't wear the right accent, the right alumni badge, the right skin, or the right silence - you become a threat before you become a story.

But here's the plot twist:

That *no* didn't destroy me.

It **defined** me.

Because in that rejection, I met a version of myself I hadn't seen before - the one who didn't ask for permission anymore. The one who realized that acceptance is sweet, but it's not required. The one who decided to build doors instead of waiting for someone else to open one.

That *no* became fuel.

And every success since then - every project I led, every team I built, every idea that finally saw the light of day - carries the fingerprints of that rejection

So if you're reading this at your lowest, remember this:

Rejection isn't the opposite of validation - it's the birthplace of reinvention.

The world will say no again and again.

But you - you decide what happens next.

Because *being determined doesn't mean you don't get hurt.*

It means you *move anyway.*

Chapter 3: Resilience Has No Manual

Picking myself up when there's no script, no mentor, and no map - only the raw will to keep moving.

No one teaches you how to rebuild.

There's no curriculum for resilience. No on boarding guide. No HR training on how to recover when your confidence has been quietly dismantled and your sense of direction just evaporated.

You just... start walking.

Even when you don't know where it leads.

After that first big *No*, I didn't bounce back. I stumbled forward.

The worst part wasn't the rejection - it was the echo that came after. That voice in your head that doesn't just question your skills, it questions your sense of self. "What if this is it?" "What if they're right?" "What if I've peaked and didn't even know it?"

And that's the moment you realize:

Success is loud.

But healing is quiet.

You can't post it. You can't perform it. You just live it - one uneasy breath, one bruised step, one small, unsexy act of showing up.

I began to study failure like it was a science.

Not the failure they glamorize in startup TED Talks.

But the kind that costs you months of sleep and erodes your edges.

I watched people who survived - not the most talented, not the most connected, but the most **anchored**. They had something under the surface. And I knew I had to build my own version of that - whatever it was.

For me, it began with a decision:

“I will outlast this.”

Not outshine. Not outperform.

Outlast.

So I built systems where there were none.

- I created structure in my day, even when my confidence was in pieces.
- I reached out to people, not to ask for help - but to learn.
- I read. A lot. Not for inspiration, but for perspective - Stoicism, strategy, sociology. I wasn’t chasing motivation. I was building *mental architecture*.

And slowly, the ground under me began to harden. Not into comfort, but into clarity.

That’s when I learned something most people miss:

Resilience is not born in the moment you get back up.

It’s born in the decisions you make while you're still on the floor.

Do you numb out? Or do you lean in?

Do you retreat into bitterness? Or rebuild with boundaries?

I chose to rebuild - brick by bloody brick.

Not because I felt strong. But because staying down wasn’t an option.

Years later, people would ask, "How did you bounce back so fast?"

And I'd smile, knowing the truth:

I didn't bounce.

I crawled.

Then walked.

Then sprinted.

Then soared.

But I never forgot what it felt like to stand at the rock bottom with no map and no momentum.

That memory became my compass.

So if you're in that space right now - the in-between, the fog - let this chapter remind you:

There is no manual for resilience.

But there is movement.

And movement becomes momentum.

Even the smallest step forward is a refusal to be deterred.

Chapter 4: The Quiet Fight for Identity

The invisible battle to be seen, respected, and understood - across cultures, accents, and expectations.

No one warned me that identity would be a negotiation.

Not an inheritance. Not a banner to wave. But a constant, quiet negotiation - of how much to show, how much to hide, and how much to edit in order to "belong."

When I first stepped into global rooms - whether in the US, the UK, or the Philippines - I brought with me more than experience. I brought **accents**, **habits**, and **codes** that weren't listed on my résumé but shaped how people received me.

And it was here, not in childhood, that I learned what it really means to be *foreign*.

Not just because of where you're from - but because of what you refuse to let go of.

My grammar was perfect. My logic was sharp.

But in rooms where presence meant polished ease and informal power, I realized quickly:

Intellect doesn't always earn you respect.

Sometimes familiarity does and sometimes mimicry.

I remember a specific moment in London.

A meeting with senior stakeholders - all sharp suits, clipped confidence, and eyes that scanned for weakness. I had the data. The roadmap. The strategy. But I didn't have *their comfort*. My accent made them lean in - not with interest, but suspicion. My directness, shaped by a training culture back home, came off as "aggressive." My silence in certain moments - respect, in my context - was read as uncertainty.

I wasn't just presenting a deck. I was auditioning for acceptance.

And in that moment, I saw clearly: the fight wasn't just external.

It was internal.

The temptation to assimilate, to soften, to shrink… just to fit in.

But here's the thing: **I didn't come this far to wear a costume.**

That day, I chose something dangerous: authenticity.

Not the loud, rebellious kind. But the consistent, unshakable kind.

I spoke less but with precision.

I stopped apologizing for not being "one of them."

And slowly - quietly - something shifted.

Respect doesn't always come instantly.

But **authenticity compounds**.

And over time, it builds something performance never can: **trust**.

I also learned that **identity isn't just what you preserve - it's what you refine**.

I didn't cling to pride. I evolved with purpose.

I sharpened my language. I studied cross-cultural nuance.

Not to impress, but to connect.

Because adaptation isn't surrender. It's strategy.

You can carry your roots and still extend your reach.

In the Philippines, the lesson was different - subtler.

There, I wasn't a foreigner. I was a hybrid - respected, but also expected to stay within certain frames. I saw the brilliance of local talent, yet how often it was overlooked. I saw voices dimmed, not because of ability, but because of a system that taught people to wait their turn - sometimes forever.

It broke something in me.

And it gave birth to something else: **a commitment to visibility.**

Not just for myself - but for those who never got in the room.

So yes, this chapter is personal. But it's also political.

Because the fight for identity isn't about ego - it's about agency.

To be who you are *and* be respected for it.

To lead without erasing your story.

To walk into any room and bring your full self - not a filtered version.

You don't owe the world a version of you that makes it comfortable.

You owe the world your *integrity*.

And the sooner you stop editing your essence, the sooner your identity becomes your superpower - not your struggle.

But as I stepped back into the world - no longer broken, but not yet fully transformed - I began noticing something deeper.

The chaos around me hadn't changed. But I had.

And what I saw next would alter how I viewed every system I ever stepped into.

Chapter 5: The Pattern Beneath the Pattern

There's a moment when experience stops teaching you and starts revealing patterns.

After the rebuild, after I found my footing again, I stepped back into the world -no longer broken, but not yet fully transformed.

The chaos hadn't changed. The complexity hadn't lessened. But something had shifted in me.

What once overwhelmed me now began to unfold in slow motion. I could see what was happening… and why.

And what I saw next would alter how I viewed every system I ever stepped into.

At first, it was just a feeling - that familiar dysfunction seemed to echo across industries, geographies, even job roles.

What looked different on the surface felt uncannily similar underneath.

A broken on boarding process in one country felt like the fractured communication loop I'd seen in another.

A toxic leadership culture in one vertical sounded like the hollow incentive plan in a different one.

It wasn't the language or the technology that linked them - it was the pattern beneath the pattern.

And I started asking myself:

> *What if failure isn't unpredictable?*
>
> *What if it's designed into the system - quietly, invisibly, by default?*

I went back through projects I'd helped rebuild, cultures I'd watched fracture, and orgs. I'd seen rise and collapse.

And the more I looked, the more consistent the fractures became.

I wasn't looking at people anymore. I was looking at design.

Gallup found that only **21% of employees strongly agree that their performance is managed in a way that motivates them to do outstanding work**. That's not just a failure in process - it's a breakdown in belief.

According to **Deloitte**, while **76% of global executives** say they're actively redesigning the work environment, fewer than **30% feel ready to lead those changes effectively**. The will is there, but the systems often lag behind.

And **McKinsey** has long reported that **70% of transformation efforts fail** - not because the strategies are flawed, but because the culture is misaligned and trust is never built.

I didn't need a research paper to know that.

I'd already seen it in real life, again and again.

I was once asked to evaluate a newly acquired business unit. Revenue was falling. Attrition was climbing. Net Promoter Scores were flat.

Everyone pointed to broken training and hiring misfires. But the real issue wasn't downstream. It was upstream.

Feedback went unacknowledged. Recognition was cosmetic. The people closest to the problem had the least say in the solution.

It wasn't broken because people didn't care.

It was broken because the system made caring costly.

I started scribbling in my notebooks - loops, failure modes, soft systems thinking.

What began as field notes slowly turned into frameworks.

I began seeing three core fractures in nearly every struggling environment I touched:

1. **Broken trust loops** - where leaders request feedback, then vanish.
2. **Misaligned incentives** - where performance metrics compete with purpose.
3. **Institutional gaslighting** - where dysfunction is tolerated as long as the optics look good.

I wasn't reacting anymore. I was diagnosing.

I wasn't just fixing. I was decoding.

This wasn't about restoring what had been.

This was about *designing what hadn't yet existed.*

By the time I started seeing the patterns clearly, I wasn't just rebuilding. I was reimagining.

Not because I had the authority.

But because I had the lens.

And that lens changed everything.

It showed me that most organizations aren't broken because of people.

They're broken because of what's invisible - misaligned time horizons, culture masquerading as compliance, success metrics that ignore lived experience.

This chapter of my journey didn't give me all the answers.

But it gave me a question I would carry into every boardroom, training lab, or founding team I'd work with after:

> *What if we could design for integrity from the start?*

Not by reacting faster - but by recognizing sooner.

Not by forcing control - but by enabling clarity.

Not by chasing outcomes - but by correcting architecture.

And with that lens, I stopped leading by instinct alone.

I started leading by insight.

I wasn't playing catch-up anymore.

I was positioning the board.

Chapter 6: Where Culture Meets Consequence

Some people still call it "the soft stuff."

Culture. Values. Belief systems.

They're fine for on boarding decks and leadership retreats - but when it's crunch time, they say, it's execution that matters.

They're wrong.

I've lived in high-output, high-pressure environments across sectors and geographies.

And every time an operation faltered, every time a transformation failed, every time a team unraveled -the root cause wasn't the execution.

It was the culture behind it.

I was once told:

"Culture's important, Joel - but let's focus on delivery first."

And I remember thinking:

Delivery is a downstream consequence.

Culture is the pipeline.

You don't lose a client because of one bad email.

You lose them because your team never learned how to close a gap.

Because feedback died somewhere inside a system that looked efficient but was emotionally disconnected.

You don't lose talent because the salary wasn't enough.

You lose them because their work had no echo - no signal that it mattered.

Because the culture rewarded performance but never taught people how to feel proud of it.

Culture isn't the soft stuff.

It's the infrastructure underneath everything.

From Words to Workflows

At one point, I helped lead a redesign of a training division inside a struggling unit.

On the surface, it was about optimizing on boarding, refining the curriculum, driving down time-to-productivity.

But underneath?

We had to rebuild trust.

New hires didn't believe the system worked for them.

Managers were burned out on policy over people.

The story the company told in its brochures wasn't the one they were living.

So we anchored on one principle: **Clarity.**

We rewrote the playbooks.

Installed post-mortem rituals, even for wins.

Built micro-coaching feedback into the daily rhythm, not just the quarterly review.

And something shifted.

People began to talk about mistakes without fear.

Managers stopped asking, “Did you hit the number?” and started asking, “What helped or hindered it?”

New hires got up to speed in a third of the time.

No one mentioned “culture.”

But it was the difference between dysfunction and flow.

The Culture Stack: Belief → Behavior → Business Impact

Every organization runs on this stack - whether they admit it or not:

1. **Belief** – what the organization claims to value
2. **Behavior** – what actually gets reinforced
3. **Norms** – the patterns that form over time
4. **Impact** – the results that emerge from all of it

If you don’t intentionally architect that stack, it will form itself - and often in ways that work against your mission.

In high-performing environments I’ve built, this became my model:

> “Translate belief into behavior.
>
> Codify behavior into design.
>
> Let design shape daily decisions.
>
> And let those decisions generate durable outcomes.”

Culture is not theory.

It’s systematized humanity.

Execution without Soul Is just Efficiency

I used to chase efficiency like it was the highest goal.

How fast can we train?

How many tickets can we close?

How tight can we script the escalation?

But I've seen efficient systems that left teams numb.

And I've seen human-centered cultures that turned performance around with fewer tools and lower budgets - because people cared.

Here's what I believe now:

> Execution without soul is just efficiency.
>
> But when culture and execution are aligned - impact becomes inevitable.

That's where I began to shift again.

Not just from fixing broken patterns,

but from **engineering alignment** between values, actions, and outcomes.

I wasn't managing anymore.

I was composing.

And in that rhythm - belief feeding behavior feeding results -

I found what leadership could feel like when it was both *deliberate and alive.*

Now, the question wasn't just:

What's broken?

It was:

What belief is missing in this system - and how do I design it back in?

That's when I stopped reacting to the moment.

And started playing for the pattern ahead.

I had finally seen it clearly: culture isn't just what people say or celebrate. It's what guides their hands under pressure.

And once I understood that, I stopped trying to manage outcomes... and started designing for inevitability.

Part II:
The Fire:
The tests that refine, not destroy

Chapter 7: Chess, Not Checkers- The shift from reactive leadership to strategic foresight.

When leadership shifts from reacting to strategizing. This chapter unpacks how I begin seeing patterns, not just problems - and how I learned to lead with foresight, not force.

By the time I began thinking in terms of inevitability, I realized I wasn't reacting anymore.

I was reading patterns, placing pieces, shaping pressure - not just responding to it.

I wasn't playing checkers in real time. I was playing chess with foresight.

There's a moment in every leader's life when instinct stops being enough.

You realize the moves that once won you praise are no longer working. You've mastered the tactical - the to-dos, the turnarounds, the firefighting. But the board has changed. The stakes are higher. And it's no longer about speed.

It's about sequence.

It's about *seeing three moves ahead.*

It's about playing **chess**, not checkers.

For me, this realization came not in a leadership seminar - but in the messy reality of trying to bring clarity to chaos in industries that were moving faster than the people inside them.

I had entered roles that others had avoided.

Too political. Too broken. Too uncertain.

From JPMorgan's **fraud management systems** to leading cross-continental operations in **UK banks**, and finally to **transforming training from a cost center to a profit engine** in the BPO space - I was walking into rooms where the ceiling wasn't glass. It was *calcified tradition.*

And I knew that if I wanted to lead, I couldn't just react. I had to **reshape the board.**

The Shift: From Manager to Architect

Most leaders focus on tasks. The best focus on **ecosystems**.

I stopped looking at metrics in isolation. I started mapping **why performance lagged**, **where behavior broke down**, and **how incentives clashed with strategy**.

I realized that poor service wasn't just about weak agents. It was about **unclear onboarding**, **confusing workflows**, and **training that didn't match reality**.

So I rebuilt it.

- Trimmed bloated training modules.
- Gamified outcomes that mattered.
- Reduced onboarding from 6 months to 4 weeks.
- Watched revenue rise **15% in the very next quarter**.

This wasn't luck.

This was design.

That's chess.

The Philippine Chapter: A Masterclass in Micro-Moves

When I began leading in the Philippines, I encountered something more complex than operational inefficiency - I encountered *talent trapped in modesty.*

The team was loyal, smart, and driven.

But they had been taught to wait. To ask. To defer.

And in global operations, that hesitation is fatal.

So I engineered change - not through commands, but through culture.

- Empowered mid-level managers to make micro-decisions without top-down approval.
- Introduced mentorship tracks with KPIs that tied personal growth to business impact.
- Created a system where performance wasn't just tracked - it was *celebrated* in real-time.

Attrition dropped. NPS improved. But more than that - **people began to believe in their own authority**.

And that changed everything.

Strategic Thinking: A Survival Skill

I wasn't born with foresight. I earned it - through missteps, missed cues, and messy recoveries.

I learned to:

- Read between the lines in boardroom silence.
- Spot cultural dissonance before it erupted.

- Anticipate who would resist change - and who could champion it.
- Recognize that **data tells you what's happening; behavior tells you why.**

And in time, I didn't just manage systems. I **architected transformation**.

Because I understood that true strategy isn't about controlling every move - it's about **creating conditions where the right moves become inevitable.**

If you want applause, play checkers.

If you want legacy, play chess.

And when you do, remember:

Your job isn't just to win.

It's to redesign the board so others can win too.

Chapter 8: In the Arena

This is the moment where theory met reality. Where my reputation, credibility, and sanity were all on the line - and I had to lead not just with intelligence, but nerve.

There's a difference between leading and *being watched while you lead.*

In one, you have time to think.

In the other, every second is a test, and the room is waiting for you to flinch.

This was one of those moments.

I was handed a business unit that was, in every polite sense of the word, *failing.*

Morale was low. Numbers were lower. The client was circling - one more missed target, and the contract was gone. The team had talent but no trust. Leaders had been rotated in and out like chess pieces, each leaving behind a slightly worse version of the same broken system.

And now it was my turn.

They didn't say it outright, but I knew:

"Fix it, or fade out."

The first day in the war room, the walls were talking.

Not in words - in energy.

People sat a little too straight. Laughed a little too quickly. Gave me surface answers, hoping I wouldn't dig. But I always dig.

Because what's visible is rarely what's *real.*

What I Found

The problems weren't in the numbers. They were in the **narratives**.

- Managers were burned out from firefighting, not leading.
- Frontline staff were numbing out from scripts and SOPs that made no human sense.
- The client didn't want reports - they wanted *reassurance* that someone was finally in control.

So I did what many leaders fear:

I paused the noise and went back to the floor.

I listened - not to please, but to *diagnose*.

I shadowed the team, asking the tough questions. Walked into call recordings and stood with them in the fire.

And in that mess, I began to map the root rot.

The Turnaround

The solution wasn't cosmetic. It was structural.

I:

- **Redesigned workflows** that aligned with how the team *actually worked*, not how someone in another country assumed they should.
- **Scrapped broken KPIs** that rewarded speed over sense.

- Introduced **real-time coaching pods** with gamified feedback loops - instantly raising engagement by 50%.
- **Facilitated direct client exposure** for the team - rebuilding trust, and humanizing both ends of the table.

The Heat

But progress is never silent.

There was pushback.

From senior leaders who liked dashboards more than discomfort.

From team members afraid to change which meant more pressure.

One day, during a cross-continent call, a senior executive snapped:

"If this doesn't turn green by month-end, we'll reevaluate your leadership."

I didn't blink.

Because I knew what they didn't:

By the time the metrics turn green, the culture already has.

And I said it. Calmly. Clearly.

"We are not firefighting anymore. We are future-building. You'll get your green. But what I'm building will last longer than your quarterly window."

Silence.

Then: *"Proceed."*

The Outcome

By Q2:

- CSAT was up 24%.
- Turnover was down by almost half.
- The client, previously cold and clinical, extended the contract and publicly commended the transformation.

But those were just results.

The real win?

People believed again. Believed in themselves,in the work, andin leadership.

Anyone can lead when the sea is calm.

But in the arena - when the audience doubts you, when the air is thick with pressure, and when every move is magnified - that's when your core gets revealed.

And mine said this:

"I am not here to impress.

I am here to transform."

Chapter 9: The Betrayal Blueprint

The moments that cut deepest aren't always strategic - they're personal. This is where trust was fractured, loyalty tested, and leadership became lonely. But also where my emotional intelligence evolved and my clarity sharpened forever.

Betrayal doesn't always come with knives.

Sometimes, it comes with silence.

With polite emails. With copied CCs.

With people who once said "brother" now saying "business."

There was a time I believed loyalty was currency.

If you showed up for people, stayed late for them, backed them in front of clients, covered their gaps - they would stay in your corner when it counted.

And for a while, that belief served me.

Until it didn't.

This chapter is not about revenge.

It's not about bitterness.

It's about **awakening** - the painful but necessary kind that forces you to see people *not as they present themselves, but as they operate under pressure.*

It happened in a role that mattered.

One where I had poured not just effort, but belief. Built systems. Trained leaders. Took the hits. Raised the bar. Protected the team. Helped someone I thought would return the favor.

But when politics entered the room - **I became dispensable**.

No confrontation. Just cold maneuvers.

Sudden exclusions from key decisions.

Undermining in closed-door meetings.

And eventually, a very public distancing - dressed up in words like "realignment" and "organizational fit."

I didn't let go.

I was *displaced* - quietly.

At first, I was furious.

Not because I had lost a title,but because I had *misread the room*.

I had assumed values were shared.

That past sacrifices would be honored.

That leadership was a bond, not a bargaining chip.

But here's what betrayal teaches you:

"Never confuse shared goals with shared principles."

Some people are with you because it suits them.

Not because they believe in you.

The Emotional Debrief

After the dust settled, I did something many don't.

I didn't move on.

I moved *inward*.

I asked myself:

- What signs did I ignore?

- Where did I overextend without boundary?
- Why was I afraid to confront earlier?

And the hardest one:

What did this betrayal come to teach me?

The Rebuild

I didn't become colder.

But I became clearer.

- I now *watch patterns more than promises.*
- I *document trust the way others document performance.*
- I lead with openness, but I **don't delegate integrity checks.**

I also learned this:

Forgiveness isn't about freeing them.

It's about freeing yourself to move forward without carrying their shadow.

Years later, I crossed paths with that same individual.

No drama. No confrontation. Just clarity.

They asked, lightly, "Hope there are no hard feelings?"

I smiled.

"No hard feelings. Just hard boundaries."

Every betrayal is a blueprint.

Not for revenge.

But for how to build wiser next time.

And if you're leading for the long haul, you'll need both -

the scars and the standards.

Chapter 10: Building in the Dark

This is the stretch of my journey when everything slowed down - visibility, validation, even hope. But beneath the surface, you were planting foundations so deep, they'd one day become unshakable. This is a chapter for anyone still waiting to be seen.

Everyone celebrates the comeback.

No one documents the *quiet* years.

The years when there are no LinkedIn announcements.

No headhunters calling.

No one checking in "just to see how you're doing."

Just… silence.

After the betrayal - and the restructuring that quietly shoved me out of the frame I helped to build - I found myself in unfamiliar terrain.

No crisis.

No chaos.

Just an eerie stillness.

It was the kind of professional twilight where nothing's *wrong*, but nothing feels *right* either.

I still had the skills. Still had the experience.

But something in me had shifted.

I wasn't looking for a title.

I was looking for **alignment**.

And that kind of search doesn't happen in the spotlight.

It happens in the shadows - **where most people give up.**

The Invisible Work

In those months - maybe even years - I became a builder again.

But not of titles.

Of *systems.*

Of *thought frameworks.*

Of *principles* I'd never violate again, even if it cost me popularity.

I designed:

- Training models that compressed ramp-up time by months.
- Career progression maps for frontline workers who were always overlooked.
- Customer experience metrics that connected empathy with enterprise impact.

No one was watching.

But I wasn't building for applause.

I was building **so that when the moment came, I'd be undeniable.**

Personal Growth Nobody Claps For

In that season, I:

- Learned deeply - not just business books, but philosophy, behavioral science, even theology.
- Watched how people *truly* grow - not from pressure, but from safety and belief.

- Unlearned my addiction to urgency. Replaced it with **intentionality**.

There's a strange power that comes when no one is checking your progress.

You start building **for depth, not display**.

"What Are You Working On These Days?"

It's the question that used to sting.

fFor a while, I had no impressive answer.

Just quiet experiments.

Thought leadership drafts.

Mentoring sessions no one knew about.

And frameworks that hadn't been published - yet.

But now I understand:

If you're doing real work, the world won't always understand it at first.

That's not a problem.

That's a sign.

The Turning Point

The turning point didn't arrive with fanfare.

It came through a single phone call.

Someone who had seen my quiet work - observed how the systems *actually worked*, how people *actually grew* under my leadership - reached out.

"I heard you're the one who rebuilt that program.

We're building something ambitious - and I don't want noise. I want depth."

That one call unlocked everything that followed.

Not because I had chased it.

But because I had become **ready for it**.

Some of your greatest work will happen in obscurity.

Do it anyway.

Because the day will come when someone calls.

And you won't need to scramble.

You'll just smile and say,

"I've been preparing for this."

Chapter 11: When Fire Became Fuel

Every scar, setback, and silent sacrifice suddenly becomes useful. This chapter captures that pivotal moment - a quiet victory that didn't just validate my journey, but crystallized my purpose.

They say the comeback is sweeter than the climb.

But what they don't say is that **you rarely know you're in it when it begins.**

It doesn't arrive with fireworks.

It arrives quietly - *in a meeting, in a message, in a problem that everyone's afraid to touch but you feel oddly drawn to.*

I remember the call clearly.

"We've tried everything. The team's disengaged. NPS is flat. The training program is bloated, and honestly, we don't even know what we're measuring anymore."

They weren't asking for a trainer.

They were asking for a *fixer.*

Someone who could step into the fire and find structure, soul, and sanity - fast.

They didn't know it, but **I had been preparing for this** in the dark for years.

This wasn't just another gig.

This was a *reckoning.*

Entering the Fire

From the outside, the project looked like every other transformation mandate - Optimize training. Cut costs. Improve output. Retain talent.

But underneath it, I saw the real battle:

- No one trusted the system.
- The training had become a checkbox, not a catalyst.
- Leaders were tired. Learners were numb.
- And frontline staff - the heartbeat of the business - felt disposable.

And that's where I found my fuel.

Because **I had once been dismissed. Silenced. Burned out.**

Now I had a chance to *rewrite that story for others.*

The Rebuild

I didn't pitch another playbook. I **rewired the entire learning philosophy**.

- We collapsed 6 months of generic onboarding into **4 weeks of power learning** - immersive, real-world, human-centered.
- Gamified knowledge retention - not with gimmicks, but with *emotionally resonant stories and feedback loops.*
- Built internal mentorship tracks and linked them to *career pathways*, not just training scores.

- Created a **real-time dashboard** that measured more than compliance - it measured growth, confidence, and engagement pulse.

The Shift

What happened next wasn't just operational. It was cultural.

- **Productivity rose 25%.**
- **New hire performance jumped 35%.**
- **Revenue uptick of 15%** - not in the quarter after training. *In the very next one.*
- But most importantly - people started *believing* again.

And that's the part I remember the most.

Not the numbers.

The looks on people's faces when they realized, *"I'm not just a number here."*

What That Fire Taught Me

I used to think strength was born from pressure.

Now I know:

> **Strength is born when pain finds a purpose.**
>
> **When the very thing that hurt you becomes the very thing that fuels your healing of others.**

This wasn't just a win.

This was *closure.*

And *beginning.*

A quiet, inner voice said:

"This is what you were meant for."

Not applause.

Not titles.

But *transformation.*

There will be a moment in your life where all the wounds, the waiting, the whispered doubts - suddenly make sense.

That moment won't come for revenge.

It will come for redemption.

And when it does, you'll know:

You weren't just built to survive fire.

You were meant to carry light through it.

Part III:
The Compass:
What remains when the applause fades.

Chapter 12: Purpose Over Prestige

Not every opportunity is a blessing. Some are distractions. This chapter explores the rare courage it takes to walk away - from titles, money, or visibility - because they don't align with my truth.

In a world obsessed with optics, **turning something down feels like treason.**

Treason against ambition.

Against momentum.

Against the unspoken rule that says: *if it looks good, take it.*

But I've learned something:

> **The wrong "yes" will cost you more than a thousand "nos."**

The offer was shiny.

Big title. Big cheque. High-visibility role.

The kind that gets press releases, not just promotions.

But something about it didn't sit right.

Not because I doubted my ability.

But because I could see **what they really wanted**:

- A figurehead, not a force.
- A resume with shine, not a soul with direction.
- A leader who would uphold the illusion of transformation - but not challenge the machinery underneath.

They didn't want *change*.

They wanted *compliance dressed as innovation*.

And I had spent too long building integrity to sell it off for visibility.

The Inner Conflict

Make no mistake - walking away wasn't easy.

I thought of everything:

- What people would say.
- The optics of rejecting a prestigious role.
- The "what ifs" that haunt every leader trying to stay aligned.

But deep down, I knew:

This wasn't growth.

It was glorified distraction.

And sometimes the most strategic move you can make is *not playing the game at all.*

What I Chose Instead

I chose projects that didn't make headlines but changed lives.

I chose work where I could:

- Architect cultures, not just strategies.
- Elevate invisible talent, not just manage stars.
- Build systems where people could rise, not just perform.

I chose depth over dopamine.

Impact over illusion.

Purpose over prestige.

The Aftermath

Some people were confused.

Some judged.

Some quietly applauded.

But what mattered most was this:

I slept better.

I worked freer.

I created bolder.

Because when your compass is internal, *external applause becomes optional.*

Not every ladder leads upward.

Some lead nowhere - just higher up in someone else's dream.

So pause and ask yourself:

"Is this taking me closer to who I want to become - or just further into who I'm expected to be?"

And if the answer is misaligned, don't hesitate.

Walk.

Walk with grace.

Walk with power.

Walk with purpose.

Because prestige fades.

But purpose compounds.

Chapter 13: The Operating Layer

Thirteen truths I bled for, that became the system behind the system

There comes a point in leadership where belief isn't enough.

If you can't build it into something that outlives your presence, it was never leadership - it was performance.

I didn't want applause.

I wanted a system that could **carry clarity without me in the room**.

Not charisma. Not force. Not dependency.

Architecture.

These aren't strategies from a slide deck.

These are truths I carved out of conflict, burnout, redesign, and the slow art of learning to lead humans, not just functions.

This is the **operating layer** - not process, but *philosophy, designed to move*.

1. People don't burn out from work. They burn out from meaninglessness.

We started treating "lack of purpose" as a performance blocker - because it was.

Every initiative began with a "Why it matters" briefing. Not to inspire - but to **anchor**.

2. Structure is not control. It's dignity.

Ambiguity is where blame grows.

We made structure sacred - not as restriction, but as respect.

Clear expectations. Clear ownership. Clear consequence.

3. Unclear rituals create hidden hierarchies.

We made bold rituals . Weekly resets. Ownership handoffs.

Everyone knew where they stood, how decisions landed, and what mattered.

It wasn't about equality. It was about **visibility**.

4. Loyalty isn't about retention. It's about recognition.

People didn't stay for perks. They stayed for the feeling of being **irreplaceably seen**.

Not "good job." But: *"What you did today now lives in our culture."*

5. Speed is addictive - and often dishonest.

We learned to interrogate urgency.

We moved fast, but never skipped *clarity checks.*

Slowness isn't the enemy. **False momentum is.**

6. Psychological safety is not a vibe. It's a system.

We didn't just encourage dissent - we designed for it.

Structured response windows. Optional anonymity. Post-mortems that asked, "What did we ignore?"

Safety wasn't emotional. It was **engineered**.

7. Culture is what people protect when leadership isn't watching.

So we asked: *"What, if removed, would break our team's heart?"*

That's where our values lived. We didn't invent them.

We listened for them.

8. What gets repeated becomes belief.

Wins weren't enough. We celebrated *how* we won.

Behavior became culture. Culture became reflex.

Reflex became rhythm.

9. Unspoken tension is the most expensive kind.

Avoided issues cost trust.

We surfaced misalignments early - not as conflict, but as calibration.

10. Discussion, not confrontation - tension is not the enemy.

Most dysfunction doesn't come from disagreement. It comes from people fearing disagreement.

We turned dissent into **design fuel**:

- "What are we not aligned on yet?"
- "What's being left unsaid?"
- "What would you do differently if you weren't afraid?"

We didn't demand consensus.

We demanded **truth, respectfully delivered**.

Because when people are free to disagree, systems evolve.

11. Design for transfers, not just tasks.

We built continuity into everything.

From handover documents to embedded wisdom reviews, no success was allowed to vanish with the person who led it.

12. Leadership isn't what you teach. It's what your system permits.

If people couldn't lead without being loud, political, or favored - the system was broken.

So we rebuilt it.

13. The real metric: Do people act like this place is theirs?

Ownership is not just initiative.

It's **unprompted care**.

It's changing what's broken without needing permission.

And when it showed up, we didn't call it extraordinary.

We called it **working as intended**.

By this point, I knew I wasn't building a company.

I was building an **operating layer that held human clarity inside system rhythm**.

People didn't follow because I convinced them.

They stayed because they felt **what we had built was now theirs to protect**.

They weren't just employees.

They were the **inheritors of integrity**.

Not because I asked them to be.

But because the system we built made it natural to stay.

Chapter 14: The Equation Beneath the Culture

Culture isn't chemistry. It's math. Not cold math - human math. And like any real equation, it shows you what creates stability… and what slowly erodes it.

Most people talk about culture like it's a feeling.

Like it's either there or it isn't.

But I've come to believe culture is more like **a living equation** - made up of visible behaviors, unseen assumptions, and moments no one claps for.

Not theoretical. Not abstract.

Just real patterns, real relationships, and how long you're willing to protect them.

The Culture Equation

C = (V × A × R) ÷ U

Where:

- **C** = *Cultural strength and consistency*
- **V** = *Visible values* - what leaders do, not what posters say
- **A** = *Accountability* - whether people follow through, and if consequences are fair
- **R** = *Relationship refresh* - how often people reconnect honestly
- **U** = *Unspoken buildup* - the small resentments, misalignments, and silences that pile up over time

---

What It Means in Real Life

Every strong team I've led had **visible values** - not in orientation decks, but in decisions.

You knew what mattered by watching who got promoted, who got corrected, and what got protected.

They also had **clear accountability**.

People weren't punished for failing - but they were called in when they ghosted a deadline or broke a cultural boundary.

Not to shame them,but to **keep the standard clean.**

And most importantly, strong cultures made time to **refresh relationships.**

I don't mean parties or all-hands.

I mean real one-on-ones.

Moments where people say:

> *"Here's what I need from you that I haven't said."*
>
> *"Here's something that's bothering me - and I don't want it to grow."*

That's what I call **refreshing trust**.

It's how relationships stop slipping quietly into tension.

The Hidden Variable: Unspoken Buildup

And here's what destroys culture faster than anything:

The things people don't say - because they think it won't matter.

The micro-resentments.

The policies no one believes in but everyone tolerates.

The people who talk in meetings but never listen after.

The behaviors that go unchecked, not because they're harmless, but because they're uncomfortable to confront.

I call this **unspoken buildup**.

And in every culture I've seen collapse - it wasn't a single betrayal.

It was months of quiet erosion, allowed to grow without a name.

So I started designing systems not just for work,

but for **clearing the air**.

Every 60 days:

- A reset check-in between team leads
- A "nudge audit" where people could surface small concerns anonymously
- A 1-question pulse: *"What's one thing we should talk about but haven't?"*

How the Equation Works

If your values are strong, and people are accountable - that's a solid start.

But if relationships are never refreshed, and if small misalignments go unspoken, your culture will still degrade.

$$\mathbf{C = (V \times A \times R) \div U}$$

The higher your **U** (unspoken buildup), the weaker your culture - even if everything else looks fine on a dashboard.

Culture isn't a tagline.

It's the result of what people ***repeat****, what they* ***tolerate****, and what they're brave enough to* ***name****.*

I used to think great culture came from alignment.

But now I know it comes from ***repair****.*

The best teams aren't the ones who get everything right.

They're the ones who talk about it when they don't.

Chapter 15: The People Who Stayed

This chapter is a tribute. Not to the loudest supporters, but to the quiet constants. The ones who reminded you of who you were when you forgot. The ones who didn't just clap for your wins - they stood beside you in your wreckage.

Every leader has a highlight reel.

But every human has a support system.

And in the moments when the lights dimmed, the stage disappeared, and I questioned if I could keep going - they were there.

Not always with advice.

Not always with solutions.

But always with *presence*.

And presence, in its purest form, is power.

My Father - Discipline Without Drama

He never needed to say much.

A veteran. A man of few words. But every word he chose felt like a blueprint.

I watched him face life's unpredictability with a spine of steel and a silence that taught me strength isn't volume - it's *consistency*.

When I doubted my worth, he didn't fix it.

He just *stayed*.

Reminding me with his stillness that **dignity doesn't shout - it simply stands its ground.**

The Friend Who Never Forgot Me

There was a season when I disappeared.

Work failed. Deals collapsed. I became a ghost in my own life.

Most people let the silence grow.

But this one friend - who had nothing to gain, no agenda - checked in.

Every week. Sometimes with words. Sometimes with memes. Sometimes just a "Still here if you are."

I later told them, "You didn't say anything profound."

They replied, *"I didn't need to. You just needed to know you weren't invisible."*

They were right.

The Teammate Who Saw Me

In one of my toughest leadership seasons - where targets were brutal and trust was low - I had a teammate who didn't just *work for me*, they *believed with me*.

When systems broke, they built patches.

When people left, they stayed late.

When I lost confidence, they quietly carried the culture until I could carry it again.

You don't forget people like that.

Because they didn't stay out of obligation.

They stayed because they saw your soul *beneath the strategy.*

My Inner Circle - The Quiet Backbone

They never needed credit.

They never posted about it.

But they picked me up after every "no."

Listened to every plan I wasn't ready to launch.

Held space for dreams that sounded impossible.

They reminded me:

"You are not what the world applauds. You are what you continue building when it forgets to watch."

We celebrate the stars.

But let's not forget the sky they shine against.

The people who held us when we were too tired to hold ourselves: they are your sky.

So if you have one - even just one - person who stays when it's hard, when it's slow, when you're not impressive...

Thank them.

Honor them.

And when your time comes - be that person for someone else.

Because in the end, success is sweet.

But being truly seen?

That's sacred.

Chapter 16: Involved Until Resolved

This is the soul of my journey. The principle that outlived titles, roles, countries, and seasons. Not just a mindset - a way of life: never abandon the problem, the person, or the principle until it's made whole.

Some people lead for applause.

Some for legacy.

And some because they simply **cannot look away**.

That's me.

Not because I'm fearless.

But because I *refuse to walk away unfinished.*

I've been called many things in my career -

Dedicated. Stubborn. Unreasonable.

But the truth is simpler than any of those labels:

If I put my name to something - I stay with it.

If I start a problem - I stay in it.

If I see pain - I don't flinch from it.

Whether it's a broken system, a misunderstood employee, a crumbling culture, or a client on the verge of collapse - I don't back off at the first sign of discomfort.

I go deeper.

I stay longer.

I remain… ***involved. Until resolved.***

It's Not a Tagline. It's a Vow.

I've watched leaders solve for the short term:

- Patch the KPI, but not the root cause.
- Dismiss the difficult employee without understanding the trigger.
- Shift blame upward, downward, sideways - anywhere but inward.

But I've also watched what happens when someone **stays**.

Stays in the feedback loop.

Stays in the coaching.

Stays in the *messy middle* - long after the headlines fade.

That's where trust is born.

That's where loyalty compounds.

That's where culture is rewritten.

Some principles are chosen.

This one revealed itself - through the hardest seasons, the quietest decisions, and the most ordinary moments that somehow shaped everything.

"Involved Until Resolved" isn't a strategy.

It's what I defaulted to **when I had no title to lean on.**

It's what remained when every other system failed.

It's the one part of me that never needed rebranding.

You've seen pieces of it across this book:

- In Chapter 4, when I rebuilt instead of blamed

- In Chapter 6, when I refused to patch culture with platitudes
- In Chapter 10.5, when I turned patterns into permanence
- In Chapter 11, when I honored the ones who stayed

But this isn't a recap.

It's a closing truth.

A principle that didn't start as a mantra - it started as **instinct**.

And then became **choice**.

And now, it's my system.

Where the Principle Got Proven

No spotlight.

No headline.

Just a room with tension, a moment no one wants to own, and a decision no one's brave enough to wait for.

That's where "Involved Until Resolved" lives.

It lives in the moment you feel your gut say:

> *"This is yours. Stay in it. See it through."*

It's not loud. It's not glossy.

But it's where real change grows roots.

The Philosophy in Action

Let me take you to six moments.

Not case studies. Not hero stories.

Just the truth of what I learned because I stayed - and what happened because I didn't flinch.

1. The Quiet Exit That Wasn't About Pay

It was a good employee.

The one everyone relied on, but no one realized had started drifting.

I could've accepted the usual HR write-up: "seeking new growth."

But something felt off.

So I stayed.

Read every exit interview that quarter.

Sat in peer calls. Talked to people *after* hours.

What emerged?

A pattern.

New hires didn't feel seen in the first 30 days.

They were onboarded to tasks, not to *trust.*

We changed everything:

- Early leadership signal calls
- A "Belonging Check" in week 2
- Rewrote the first 45-day rhythm for managers

Attrition dropped.

But more than that - new hires *stayed emotionally engaged*, not just employed.

Resolution wasn't an intervention.

It was **design powered by presence**.

2. The Performance Review That Should've Been a Goodbye

A mid-level manager under-delivered for three cycles.

Smart. Loyal. But slipping.

I was advised to replace him.

But I stayed.

Met him offsite. No slides. No blame.

What came out was shame.

He'd lost belief that he could lead at this level - and no one had noticed his doubt until it calcified into underperformance.

We pulled him out of daily pressure.

Gave him a short-term delivery project, coached him in sprints.

Two quarters later, he rebuilt the very team that had lost faith in him.

Staying saved a role.

But more than that - it restored someone's inner authority.

3. The Client Who Didn't Complain, Just Drifted

No escalation.

Just a gradual erosion in tone.

Our delivery looked fine.

But they didn't feel it anymore.

Instead of dismissing it as "normal client fatigue," I went in.

Shadowed calls. Sat on frontline syncs. Asked them, simply:

"What feels off that no one's naming?"

What they said?

"You stopped listening after the renewal."

That stung. Because it was true.

We re-established a feedback rhythm.

Made the delivery cadence visible again.

Turned their ideas into product pilots.

They became our most vocal champions a year later.

We didn't save the account.

We saved the **relationship behind the metrics.**

4. The Re-org That Could've Broken People

It was logical. It made sense on paper.

But I could feel it in my team - *the trust fracture.*

Rather than push through, I paused rollout.

Brought affected teams into design.

Not to ask permission - but to let them shape the transitions that would affect their futures.

We lost a month.

But we gained *five years' worth* of internal goodwill.

Staying in discomfort allowed us to **design transformation with consent - not compliance.**

5. The Personal Season Where I Almost Checked Out

There was a quarter when I was done.

Not in words. Just in energy.

Things were working, but not lighting me up.

And I was ashamed to admit it - because I was the leader.

I stayed anyway.

Not to fake it.

But to re-immerse myself in conversations that mattered.

Not dashboards. People. Purpose.

And slowly - clarity returned.

This wasn't about performance anymore.

It was about confronting the parts of myself I had quietly abandoned.

6. The System That Needed One More Week

We were launching a new reporting workflow.

Deadline locked. Ops ready.

But I knew it wasn't *clean.*

There were handoffs which were still fuzzy. One metric definition still inconsistent.

Everyone said ship.

But I stayed.

We held the release. Reclarified. Pressure-tested.

That one week saved us 200 hours of downstream QA effort.

Everyone called it perfectionism.

But I knew it was about coherence - protecting the structure before chaos needed fixing.

What It Means Now

"**Involved Until Resolved**" is no longer just something I do.

It's the filter that defines what I lean into, what I walk away from, and what

choose to carry all the way through.

It's how I've learned to measure maturity - in people, in systems, and in myself.

Because anyone can show up at the start.

But real leadership is what you do **after the urgency fades** and the silence begins.

How I Built It into My Systems

Presence doesn't scale.

But values can.

So I began baking this principle into the structure:

- Every project closes with a "shadow loop" - *what still feels unresolved emotionally, not just operationally?*
- Manager reviews include a line item: "What decision did you exit too fast?"
- Handoffs aren't complete until there's clarity, not just delivery

I didn't want to be the only one who stayed.

I wanted to lead in a way that taught **others how to stay meaningfully** - and then taught the system to hold that expectation without needing me in the room.

You can be respected for your brilliance.

Admired for your strategy.

Promoted for your performance.

But you'll be remembered for the things you stayed with - and the way you stayed.

I've stayed long enough to know that most outcomes fade - but presence leaves an imprint.

Not in applause, but in the way people remember how you made them feel when it mattered most.

So if you've come this far in the book, here's my final offering:

Don't lead like you're passing through.

Don't disappear just because it's no longer trending.

Don't build fast what you're unwilling to fix slow.

Stay in it.

Own it.

Walk with it until it's clean.

Stay until it's resolved.

And in that presence, your legacy will be louder than anything you ever posted.

Chapter 17: Determined, Not Deterred

This is the declaration. The soul-stamp. A final reckoning with every storm faced and every stand taken. It's not about being fearless - it's about refusing to be moved by fear.

People often ask,

"What keeps you going?"

Not as a polite question - but as a real one.

Because by now they've seen the weight.

The betrayals.

The broken systems.

The brilliant ideas that were too early.

The wins no one clapped for.

The rooms where you were the only one who believed in the mission.

Here's the truth:

I've been disappointed. But never defeated.

I've been slowed. But never silenced.

I've lost deals, titles, support, even sleep -

but I never lost the core.

That's what this book has been about:

Keeping the core intact.

Staying in the fire without becoming it.

Fighting for what matters, even when no one is watching.

In fact, if I could sum up the kind of leadership I believe in - and the kind this book points to - it would be this:

E = M × A

Energy = Meaning × Action

Because strategy alone doesn't move people.

Meaning without motion is just sentiment.

But when the work is deeply tied to *why* it matters - and you act on it with conviction - that's when cultures shift, and people follow.

That's where the energy comes from.

Not charisma. Not noise.

But clarity - acted on.

I've learned:

That resilience isn't a personality trait. It's a practice.

That strategy is nothing without soul.

That *truth*, spoken quietly and consistently, outlasts the loudest lies.

And that is **when you lead with conviction, you will be underestimated.**

But you will never be replaceable.

Why This Book Exists

Not to impress.

Not to relive past glories.

But to say to someone - somewhere - who is quietly building their dream, quietly holding their standard, quietly refusing to give up:

You are not alone.

And you are not wrong for wanting more.

Not more titles.

But more meaning.

Not more speed.

But more *alignment*.

Final Declaration

I am not here to be liked.

I am here to be *of use*.

To build cultures, not just companies.

To design systems where people don't burn out - they rise up.

To turn every betrayal into blueprint.

To stand by those who stay.

To build in the dark.

To be involved until resolved.

To lead with heart, not performance.

And most of all…

To remain determined.

Never deterred.

🕊 Closing Reflection:

You will be tempted to compromise.

To settle. To dilute. To soften your voice.

Don't.

The world doesn't need more leaders who fit in.

It needs more who *stand out.*

More who *stay human.*

More who *stay involved.*

Let them underestimate you.

Just don't underestimate yourself.

Afterword:
A Note to the Next Builder

If you've made it to this page, you're probably someone who sees the world a little differently.

You notice the cracks in systems.

You care more than most.

You stay longer than is comfortable.

And sometimes, you wonder if the cost is worth it.

Let me tell you: **it is.**

Maybe you haven't seen the reward yet.

Maybe your breakthroughs are still buried beneath daily fires and unanswered emails.

Maybe the people around you don't fully understand what you're building, or why you refuse to compromise.

That's okay.

Because you're not building for approval.

You're building for alignment.

For dignity.

For meaning.

The world doesn't always recognize those who lead quietly.

But the people you impact - the ones who bloom because of your belief, the ones who stay because you stayed -

they see you.

And that ripple?

It goes farther than any spotlight.

So here's my ask:

- Don't rush.
- Don't shrink.
- Don't bend your values just to fit into rooms that don't deserve you.

And when the road gets dark - remember this:

The path of integrity is slower...

but it will never take you somewhere your soul can't survive.

Stay determined.

Stay involved.

Stay human.

And build what only *you* can build.

I'm rooting for you.

- *Joel Madtha*

Reflection Guide: 13 Questions for the Involved Leader

"Don't just finish the book.

Finish what it started in you."

1. The First Stand

What is one value you have refused to compromise - even when it cost you something?

2. The War Behind the Walls

Where have you seen a system fail people - and what responsibility do you feel to repair or replace it?

3. Displaced, Not Defeated

Have you ever been quietly replaced, ignored, or undervalued? How did you rebuild your sense of worth?

4. The Rebuild

What part of your life or leadership has required you to start over - and what did you carry forward into the rebuild?

5. Chess, Not Checkers

Where are you currently being invited to play the long game - and what short-term temptations are you resisting?

6. In the Arena

What is your most defining 'pressure moment'? How did you lead under that heat - and what did it reveal about you?

7. The Betrayal Blueprint

Who or what disappointed you deeply - and what boundary, belief, or blueprint emerged from that experience?

8. Building in the Dark

What are you working on right now that no one sees? Why is it still worth doing?

9. When Fire Became Fuel

What part of your pain has become a platform - a reason you show up stronger for others?

10. Purpose Over Prestige

What opportunity looked good but didn't feel right - and how did walking away grow your self-trust?

11. The People Who Stayed

Who has stayed by your side without applause or reward? What would you say to them right now?

12. Involved Until Resolved

Where in your life or work are you being called to stay - not to fix fast, but to be present until it's truly whole?

13. Determined, Not Deterred

What does "determined" mean for you now - and how will you protect that mindset in the seasons ahead?

Write. Pause. Revisit.

These questions are not meant to be rushed.

They are meant to become *your leadership mirror.*

The core held. And that was enough."

- Joel Madtha

Acknowledgments

No book - especially one this personal - is built alone.

It may carry one voice, but it's shaped by many hearts.

This is my chance to thank them.

About the Author

Joel Madtha is a leadership architect, systems thinker, and deeply human strategist known for transforming overlooked teams and untapped potential into measurable, lasting impact. With over two decades of global experience across the US, UK, India, and Southeast Asia, Joel has redefined what it means to lead with conviction in some of the world's most demanding business environments - from financial systems and training ecosystems to customer experience and operational design.

But titles aren't what define him.

What does?

His unwavering principle: **Involved Until Resolved**.

Joel has guided transformations that turned cost centers into growth engines, rewired training programs that tripled engagement, and built cultures that honored not just performance - but people.

When he's not designing human-first systems or advising leaders on high-stakes decisions, Joel writes, mentors, and builds with one goal: **to make work feel more human, and leadership feel more just.**

Determined, Not Deterred is his first book - a work born not from theory, but from trenches. It is both a testimony and a toolkit for those who still believe that values don't have to die on the way to the top.
